Jolly Roger
and the treasure

Story by Beverley Randell

Illustrations by Chantal Stewart

Jolly Roger
went to look for treasure.

Big Pirate and Little Pirate
went, too.

"I am going to look for a box,"
said Jolly Roger.
"The treasure is in a box."

"We will look for it
here on the beach,"
said the pirates.

"Go away, Jolly Roger,"
said Big Pirate.
"We are looking here.
You go and look on the hill."

Jolly Roger went up the hill.

Away went his hat!

"My pirate hat!"

said Jolly Roger.

Jolly Roger ran after his hat.

He ran down the hill.

"Jolly Roger

is not going to find the box,"

said Big Pirate.

"We will find it,"

said Little Pirate.

13

"Here is my hat,"
said Jolly Roger.
"And look!
Here is a big box!"

"Come and see my treasure!"
shouted Jolly Roger.